THE
DANCE of LIFE

POEMS FOR THE SPIRIT

BARBARA PAUL-EMILE

EUNOIA
PUBLISHING

The Dance of Life

BARBARA PAUL-EMILE

© Barbara Paul-Emile 2005

Published by EUNOIA Publishing
1100 North 4th St. Suite 131, Fairfield, Iowa 52556

Author's Web Site: www.BarbaraPaul-Emile.com

First Edition
SoftCover ISBN: 1-59540-935-1
HardCover ISBN: 1-59540-936-X
eBook ISBN: 1-59540-937-8

This material has been written and published solely for educational purposes. The author and the publisher shall have neither liability or responsibility to any person or entity with respect to any loss, damage or injury caused or alleged to be caused directly or indirectly by the information contained in this book.

The characters and events described in this text are intended to entertain and teach rather than present an exact factual history of real people or events.

FOR SERGE
Husband, Partner, Friend

Your presence in my life is a source of
joy, love and creative strength.

Thank you for your generous loving support.

You are my "pôteau mitan,"
my strong, high, central beam.

TABLE OF CONTENTS

INTRODUCTION

The Dance of Life: Poems for the Spirit is influenced by the rich mystical shamanic heritage of the Caribbean islands and is inspired by an internal search for regenerative thought-seeds buried deep within the psyche that if discovered can lead to a deeper understanding of the layered construct of reality. The thoughts and feelings expressed in this collection reveal a personal response to the challenges faced daily as we negotiate the field of existence, moving between pain and joy, fear and love, hopelessness and triumphant overcoming.

Creative writing has always been of great interest and comfort to me. As a school girl, I wrote prose and poetry freely. However, poetry has always held a special place in my heart because the form is so beautiful, so delicate and succinct. Growing up in Springfield and Montego Bay, Jamaica, students were expected to memorize verses from the works of such English literary masters as Shakespeare, Pope, Wordsworth and Tennyson. In addition to *memory gems*, maxims taught in school in their day, my aunts and other family members could recite verses from the great classics. I remember hearing passages lovingly recited from Shakespeare's *The Tempest*. The speakers had long forgotten the source and the meaning but they remembered the words. Poetry as an oral tradition was alive and well. For my part, I loved the sound of the structured melodic phrases as they rolled off the tongue.

I recall making humble attempts and calling them songs because this designation made my compositions less ambitious. Calypso singers in the neighborhood composed songs about local happenings. In church, we sang the great Western hymns. I understood the magical power of words. The *call* and *response* pattern, which is part of the African musical legacy, was the choral form most loved in the community, especially by the grass-roots religious sects. On Sundays, one could hear the voices of the lead and response singers floating down the hills at nightfall. This pattern which allowed for greater freedom, spontaneity and richer interplay between the voices was to later influence my poetic compositions as reflected in my use of the dialogue form.

Another important development that shaped my early writing life was the receipt of my first fountain pen. I cannot explain the joy I felt at seven years old when I held this precious instrument in my hand for the first time. I received it on a Saturday evening, and after church on Sunday, I was a threat to any clear piece of paper in my household. Receiving my first fountain pen was one of the most significant occasions of my young life. Now, I could transcribe passages written in pale tremulous pencil to bright blue or black ink and I was trusted not to get ink over everything. This was the beginning of my writing life and my love for letters.

In keeping with the promise of my early interests, writing has been central to my life. I followed an academic career and have researched and written scholarly articles on a range of subjects: the English Romantic Poets, Caribbean and African American literature. I published a novel, *SEER*, set in the Caribbean in April, 2004. Poetry, however, has been a great love and a constant in my life. Regardless of the project on which I am working, I find myself writing poetry. No other form lends or molds itself as well to personal expression.

The Dance of Life: Poems for the Spirit contains poems written in response to a range of experiences both private and public. They are, for the most part, meditative and visionary in focus and explore the concerns that surface in the mind during quiet times when we withdraw from the outer world and enter a state of meditation and reflection. William Wordsworth in his Preface to the Second Edition of *The Lyrical Ballads* (1802), said that "poetry is the spontaneous overflow of powerful feelings: it takes its origin from emotion recollected in tranquility..." Building on Wordsworth's dictum, most of the poems in this collection are not only composed but conceived during times of reflection and meditation when inner and outer reality meld and one enters a deeper level of being and understanding not readily accessed by the day-to-day mind.

In my morning quiet times of inward turning, times of reaching beyond the world of convention, I center myself and reconnect with a consciousness larger than my own. I enter a state of heightened awareness and sense a creative thought-stream flow into my mind offering poetic insight into the paradoxes of life. In this state of contemplative centeredness, I oftentimes find my thoughts intertwined with memories of the subtle, mellow joys of life, remembrance of the pleasures of small things, loved things, a misty morning, the incoming tide, the elation that comes from hearing the *voice* within, the feeling of surrendering to my inner knowing, anchored by the unassailable knowledge that I am right where I am supposed to be in the world. These are all part of the sweet, sweet flow of life...

At other times, pressed by the anxieties and unresolved issues of the day, I enter a dry land of present fears and past disappointments where streams flow underground and memories of the challenges of the journey: the betrayals, the voided spaces, the broken patterns haunt and sear the mind. Yet, sustained by hope, by desire and by the relentless search for the *oneness,* the journey continues underpinned by the dogged determination to hold fast to the *tao* (way).

The poems in *The Dance of Life* bear a mystical cast that colors both imagery and verbal expression. They present an ongoing exploration in the search for meaning behind the seemingly carelessly strung multicolored beads of events that form the substance of our lives. This collection treats a range of experiences from seemingly unbearable pain and heartbreak, to successes and triumphs, culminating in the discovery of the ecstatic bands of love and deep feelings that connect us to our *Source.* The sentiments expressed in these poems also reflect the intuitive responses and the levels of internal knowing we bring to the struggles that confront us.

Several different voices can be heard in this collection. The *mythic shamanic* voice takes a wider, more comprehensive perspective on things, offering guidance, evocative admonitions and cosmic support. These shamanic poems are presented singly or in the *call* and *response* pattern where a dialogue ensues with the personality self. The *personal voice* attempts to understand and make peace with the maelstrom of private and public issues that confront us day-to-day. The *descriptive and interpretive voice* engages with the material world of people and events, and seeks to process and capture their essence and uniqueness.

The Dance of Life: Poems for the Spirit speaks to our need to value our experiences and to appreciate the richness of life in its multifacetedness. It points to a frame of reference larger than the one in which we currently exist and calls us to remembrance. It reminds us that we are part of a larger, richer construct of life than we imagined and suggests that this construct in all of its levels, layers, permutations and nuances has profound significance. It speaks to our need to grow and to become, marking us as spiritually questing beings. We are reminded that nothing we do, see or encounter is without meaning.

This collection honors our inner strength, courage, determination and the intuitive guidance that nudges us along the *way*. It promotes an enlarging of the heart, connecting us to our deeper selves and to worlds and energies beyond our immediate knowing. It is my hope that the words and images in these poems will linger in consciousness, roam the mind and nestle in the heart.

THE SPIRAL PATH:
CHALLENGES AND ADMONITIONS

The Spiral Path

This is a path that one must take alone
a path that leads to places yet unknown
a path that calls us to vistas yet unseen:

mountain tops, plateaux, rivers flowing,
    trickling streams

this is a path that leads to inner spaces quiet
    and apart
to contemplative caverns of the heart
to hidden high places of meditation
to the circle of wholeness:
                          self-integration.

Crossing Bridges

The resilience of the human spirit
is remarkable to behold,

we stumble, stagger, fall and grumbling,
    lose our way
lay in pits, exhausted by our struggles
lay forgotten, wasted, seeming dead, alone
then comes the voice from deep within
we rise, cleanse ourselves
we try again;

answering a call that comes from deep within
a voice that all have heard
a call that never will be silenced
a call that echoes down the halls of time
to find our strength, to take a risk…
to "cross the bridge"
move into selfhood
move into awareness
move into the light,

Barbara Paul-Emile

we make another try
with all our might, we hit our stride
we have the bridge in sight
swaying gently in the wind
it beckons us…

still fearful, but holding on
we take our steps
knowing: this path is right.

The Way

We grow by way of pain
By way of joy
By way of everything;

In many unseen ways
We crush the petals of our lives

Their perfumes rush to meet us
The thistles prick our feet

The path, we say is difficult
Why, only thorns are here

Petals and thistles, sweetness and pain

Life!

Barbara Paul-Emile

Woman Warrior

You are a warrior of the light
You are a beacon on a hill
You are the rallying cry of thousands
The drum that is never still;

You are the herald that signals the advance
The joy that pulses in the heart
The expression of faith made manifest
You are woman
You have withstood the test;

And...

You are loved and cared for
You are guided and you are led
Have no doubts and no regrets
There are no mistakes
You have journeyed well;

Look at the signs about you
They portend the dawn
Let go the past, move forward now
Woman,
Your time has come.

Beginnings

Opening to life
stepping over thresholds

fearlessly calling out endings,
bravely making new beginnings;

they never said it would be easy
though many believed it so;

we do not want the struggle, the pain
the transformations
we want consistency, predictability
a plan;

we want the world to stand still for us
the seasons to stay in place
the rivers to withhold their currents
the moon to hold its form;

but all things change and we with them
only the center holds
only the center holds.

Markings

No action on your path is lost
No look or smile unnoted,
No thought passes, but leaves a mark
For all is recorded;

And in my book of days and time
Your markings glisten like the sun,

For you have acted true to spirit,
True to soul,
In the midst of chaos,
You've held your own;

You've never wandered from the path
Yes, you've doubted, stayed awhile to ponder
But always, you begin again
Begin again with heart and strength
With loving resolution;

You carry my imprint in your heart
And you've never turned away
Never pretended you did not know me,
Never disowned my ways;

Rest now in your consciousness
Know your place is safe, secure and sure
Travel forth this day in full knowledge of my grace
For you are treasured, loved and valued,
I found my joy in you.

Barbara Paul-Emile

Knocking

Do not turn me away from this door
for I am a child hungry and lost
I have knocked on other doors
called out to other friends...

They were too busy to hear me
preoccupied with life's changes
their time is spent collecting, spending, having...
amassing, seeking, taking ...they follow the
sounds, the bells, the clamor;

They do not hear my call
they have no time for me
no time to listen, to hear and to heal;
so I knock on this door
do not turn me away
for I am weary, lost and weak

take me in.

Hiding Places

Come out from your hiding place
And speak to me
I welcome your presence and your voice
I seek your company
I hold you in my heart;

Dear Child, you are enough
More than enough
You are a great being, precious and strong
I salute you and I love you
Speak to me;

Let the struggle go, the pain, the fear
Speak not out of pain and sorrow,
But out of joy and strength;

Barbara Paul-Emile

I accept you,
I love you
I know you
I recognize you
I see you
I know who you are
I know why you were silent,
Forgive the harsh controllers;

Drawing strength from earth,
Water, wind and air
I empower you
Little one, you are strong,
You are loved.

Clean Slate

Feel the silence flow through you
Feel my breath upon you
Feel my love surround you
Know that you are mine;

Let go of the past
Of all that has happened or will be
Live now in the moment
On this day and in this hour;

Your slate is clean
For you have done no wrong
Let go of guilt and receive my gifts
Gifts that bring joy to your heart
And affirm life.

Barbara Paul-Emile

The Masque

See the pain reflected in the action
See the fear held in the thought
Feel the sorrow masked by laughter
See the lack of love for others
As the lack of love for self;

See the barricades are raised
See the gun-ships set to fire
Hear the emptiness in the shouting
See the trembling in the strutting
As the hollow ring of fear.

Triggers

They look to trigger their own growth,
In your clear voice, they hear their own,
In your calm presence, they think of me
In your accomplishments,
They see their preconceptions fail
They know the world to be a wider richer place
Than they had thought.

Barbara Paul-Emile

Searching...

Clay feet, clay hands,
Clay bodies,
Where are the jewels we were promised?
Where can they be found?
Beneath the clay, beneath the clay.

A Light within the Dark

Now, you feel a sadness, a hollowness and an
    emptiness, a loneliness…
But, sentinels must be inwardly sufficient
Sentinels must maintain my light within the dark
You are my sentinel, my light within the darkness
My note upon the mountain
My cascading waterfall
My beam of light among the leaves
The warmth of the morning that heralds the day
You are my morning song
The echo of my voice
Your presence makes me glad.

Vessels

My energy and power grow 'round you
My words flow from your lips
My life flows through your veins;

For you have dedicated yourself
A vessel trained for my service
I have accepted your gift;

You have crossed the river
Look not behind
Now look ahead;

There is so much more to be accomplished
So much more to share and to give
Your store will be replenished
Your light will be lit
Your breath will go out into the world
And the heavens will respond
For such is my bidding
Such is my direction
And such is your choice.

Promises

No one may take what I have given you
No thief approach, no poachers come
No greedy hands grasp or snatch the gifts
The gifts that I have given;
Or slyly, smilingly remove
Benefits bestowed;

They are yours, lady,
They are yours;

Others see them but cannot touch
They may desire but may not poach
For so it is to be;

They hear the joy ring in your voice
They feel your graceful presence
Your auric field warms them
As with a fire
But they cannot take your gifts
That cannot be;

If this were otherwise:
The mountains would lose their strength
The seas tumble on to the land
The skies fold in upon the earth
The winds run to the center of the spheres;

This cannot be, lady,
This cannot be
The gifts I have given
No one may take away.

Imprints

Do not fear your imperfections
See them as but imprints on the seas of life
The rocking of the waves
Removes all prints
Covers all with its rich flow

Feel the forgiveness of the water
Feel the gentleness of its caress
Know you are loved and cared for
Errors are all redressed

See the deep, wide ocean
See my love cover it as a mist
Feel the joy of your true being
Know all great truths are at rest.

Spirit Warrior Armed

Create an armor for yourself
For your tender spots can still be pierced
   By arrows, gunshots or the lance;

Create an armor for yourself
You interface with warriors of the world
Girded with weapons stark and piercing
Brandishing trophies on the field of battle
   Deadly trophies they have won;

Driven on by anger, fear and doubt
   They invite all comers to their bouts;

You must not accept their offer
   Turn away from their battle cries and shouts…

But when confronted, blocked, obstructed
   Turn to face them fully armed,

Helmet of undying faith and trust
Breastplate of my unwavering love
Shin-guards of intuitive self-awareness
Shield of courage, strength and grace

Draw forth your light sword;
   The sword of truth and of decision
   Hold to allegiances already made;

. . .

Hold no fear within your heart
    Be centered, bold, aligned,
Stand in the aegis of my protection
Stand in the knowing of the oneness

Expand your auric field,
    Embrace them
Say: "I have already won the day."

They hesitate in their confusion
They recall their fragmentation
    All outward show and false pretenses
    All cruel sham and false maneuvers,
            Hidden crafts and vain deceits;

They look upon the Spirit Warrior
    Standing purposeful and true
    Standing in glory as Light Warrior
    Shimmering in grand array;

And they scatter, crackling, breaking,
As the north wind blows dead leaves away.

Sentinel

I stand at the ready
my weapons sharp and clean
my eyes roving, restless
my hearing quick and keen,
I read all omens
hear all sounds
I sleep, yet I'm awake
ever, I watch
ever, I guard
ever, I protect;

Now, the castle is old and worn
the walls fall down
the stones crack
no one enters here
no one offers combat,
no one parries with the sword;

I listen for the horn
the piercing cry of battle
the summon never comes;

and I am left to tend the dying fires
to check the moat and fences
to hold to memories of bygone days;

I did not notice
the inhabitants had already left   . . .

they no longer need protection
not my weapons keen and sharp;

my strength and vigilance were their safe-keeping
my loyalty and devotion their security
now, they have spread their wings and flown away
and I am left alone;

Have I the heart to leave?

Response

I will leave this old and empty castle
I will lay my weapons down
I will walk across the portal
I will take the road to town

The sun beats upon my shoulders
The earth beneath my feet
No armor will I carry
No weapons do I need

For, I will take my freedom
Taste the fruits of my new joys
Feel the breezes brush my face
Hear the singing in the land

I will honor my own journey
Finding peace in my own way.

New Ways...

Taking your freedom is easy
It is getting to that place that is hard;

It is the stops, the turn-arounds
The anguished crying-outs
The pain...

But once you have made the journey
Once you've gotten to that place
Once you've accepted the sign
You find peace
And you are free;

Now, how do you hold your freedom?
How do you maintain your stance?
How do you forget the memories?

You release
Yes, you release
For each knows what is known
Each follows her own path
Take the wisdom and the knowing
Eat the tamarind with the honey
Take the sweetness with the sour
Access your power

. . .

And release…

Now with deliberate action
Tender guarding of soul-growth
Love yourself, love yourself
And find new ways to be,
New ways…

Soul Keepers

Your sweetness perfumes the world
Your fragrance spreads my joy
Your presence is my peace
Your constancy my altar;

Live with me in the new world,
Fear not,
Fear nothing,
For all is of me;

I but permit the learning in the world,
Be strong of courage
Be brave
Do not falter
Keep to your path;

Beloved,
Do not judge yourself
For I see all and am all
I am your heart that beats to time
Your thoughts that encompass distances
Your love that flows to all things;

I am your mind incisive and clear
I am your being serene and strong

. . .

I am your fears that move restlessly like the wind,
I am the steadiness of your spirit that
    knows the truth;

I am your courage to face each day
I am your strength, released from pain,
I am the light that surrounds your life
I am you
I AM.

Response

You are the light of every soul
the meaning of each day
the peace from which all action springs
the Source-love that creates
the goal to which we reach
the balm for every pain
the joy of every happiness
the call to rise again
You are life, reason, purpose,
You are being.

Barbara Paul-Emile

The Hero's Path

Be the hero of your life
Follow your path to the mountain-top,
Be the hero of your life
Face the dragon in the depths;

Commit to goals that stir the heart
To journeys that bid us start,
Fearlessly gaining ground each day
Knowing when to give way and when to stay;

Know when to be the warrior
    when to be the sage
Know when to be the ruler
    when to be an aide;

Access the lover without fear;
Taking courage as steps fall away…
Follow the hero's path;

Know when to move forward
    when to step back
Know when to go for changes
Accepting things you cannot change;

Know when to trust yourself
    when to listen to others

. . .

Know how to live with uncertainty
Accepting the unknown;

    Be the magician,
    the caregiver,
    the trickster,
    the wise fool,

Draw forth the thread from the labyrinthine spool
    of
    time
Be the hero of your life.

Alignment

See the sword anchored within you,
See the hilt at your heart
See the blaze of the electrifying energy
Surging forth
Create your spiritual armor;

See the insignia of the 'Threefold flame'
Nestles at your breast
Stretch forth your hand wide
See the blazing gem of blue in your right palm
The pink iridescent jewel in your left;

Hold the blue of heart and will
Hold the pink of divine love
Now you are balanced
Stable and aligned;

This is the day of days
This is the day of days.

A Love without Degrees...

Even if you did nothing in the world
Your place would be assured
Even if you said nothing in the world
Your voice would still be heard;

Even if you stayed in one place
Your energy reaches out
For you express my will
You carry my thoughts;

You are the center of my circle
You are the pounding of the Great Heart
So do not fear the changes
Do not fear the convolutions
See them, but from afar;

For you are a prophet, a sage, a seer
One who gives without return
You are my face upon the earth;

Barbara Paul-Emile

You express the great Unity
The unity that is me
You express the Great Love
A love without degrees…

So be at peace, my children
Do not fear the future
Do not regret the past
Know all things are as they should be
For you are both past and future;

Breathe the breath of Spirit
Fill your heart with joy
For only joy awaits you
How could this be otherwise?

Shamanic Voices:
Inner Dialogues

The Maker

The clay does not fear the potter
Nor the dough the baker
Nor the soil the gardener;

For each knows the hand that shapes
Knows the holy hand that nurtures
Sacred hands that heal;

Response

We know the nurturing hand that holds us, helps
us, guides us and leads us along the path. Hands
that beckon us to move beyond safe boundaries
and seek lofty heights.

hands that hold a pattern for each life.

we are that clay, that dough, that soil
in your hands, unresisting
we're molded, shaped and tilled;

in your hands we're still becoming
molecules toss and swirl within
never ending, yet beginning
pressed hard against the potter's wheel;

. . .

and the bubbles of air, the pockets of emptiness,
the weeds that grow
do not disturb our inner harmony

for all are measured and assessed
the ground is furrowed, the mold is set;

the vase emerges, glorious in its shapeliness
the bread rises knowing it is sustenance,
the soil blooms with flowers in rich largesse,
then and only then
does the shaping hand rest.

Barbara Paul-Emile

Awakening

Stop and clarify your life
Remove the clogs that stop the flow
Weed out, sift and release
So that the flow
The flow of the universe might
Come to you;

Response

I throw away my anchors
allow myself to float,
on faith intertwined with grace,

energy flows 'round me
like celestial winds
powerful in their intensity,

certain as the passage of days
strong as the crashing of the waves
sure as the pounding of ocean surf,

swirling in iridescent skies
carried on shimmering streams of light
dissolving into oneness…

. . .

Guidance

This is the day of your awakening
Live calmly and in strength
Put tardiness behind you
Live without lament
Feel my presence and my protective cloak of love
Know that I am with you always;

You need not show or prove this day
You need only BE
You need only BE;

Feel my sustaining love for you
Claim your freedom
For you are free;

Let the world and its ways go
Those who contribute must yet learn from their
    contributions
Do not be troubled or dismayed
Let my love surround you
Feel its glow, its warmth
You have the power to do all
That must be done this day.

Barbara Paul-Emile

Pebbles

Questions

Show me what I should be and
   what I should know
show me what I should become and how I should
   grow

show me who I am and who you are to me
show me my perfected form that I might be whole.

Guidance

Your fears
They are but tiny pebbles at your feet
They hurt your toes and scorch your soles
But they do not harm you;

These are but the roughness of the road
The edges sharp and jagged
Remind you of the nature of the journey
The trickiness of the path;

Stop and rest awhile
Look at the beauties along the road
Do not be distracted by annoyances.

Healing

Heal me this day
heal the breaking of my heart
heal the pain that grips and clings
held fast with taut binding strings;

help free me
from this tight embrace
help me find a better place
a wide expanse of radiant light
where at day's end
there is no night.

Guidance

Do not take it to heart
Let the pain pass
Wait to see resolutions, revolutions and changes …

You ask why they prosper
Why power is given to them
Why they wield authority
Why they seem to have the last say;

The last is not the final
They do not determine the future
So stand aside and see
Stand aside and see;

. . .

Your tears are seen and noted
We know your inner pain
Your heartache...

Remember us...
Remember, all time is one
Earth is just and does not forget
All is balanced on her turning scales;

Dry your eyes, heal your pain
We vow to you this day
That we will act on your behalf
We will remove their masks.

Barbara Paul-Emile

The Path

Be patient
Keep to the path I have shown
Your voice is mine
Your ways are mine
The path will open
My voice will sweep across the land
I will be heard
When all is ready
When all is ready.

Response

In peace this day, I follow my path
in peace this day I honor my calling
in peace this day, I affirm my true identity
let me rest in you this day
and use your strength for mine
your strength for mine.

Sometimes

Sometimes… sometimes… sometimes…
I tire of life on earth;

I tire of the stress, the strife, the wars
the jealousies large and small
the failings, the frailties and the pain
the fallings and the rising up again;

I tire of the unmaskings, the posings, the small
    treacheries
I tire of not knowing who we truly are
I tire of the search for honor, place and peace
I tire… I tire… I tire…

    yet, sometimes…
    I know why I must be here
    sometimes…
    I know why the road must be trod
    I know why we must each carry the torch
    and call to others to show the way
    sometimes…
    I know why … or think I do…
    sometimes…

but sometimes,
        I grow tired…

Barbara Paul-Emile

Guidance

It is at this time you need my strength
My unyielding fortitude and my inner
      knowing,
My subtle promptings and my eternal presence
            Call me then for I will come.

Response

Heal me, this moment, this morning
            of all the pains I carry
of all the anguish yet to be released
         heal me, heal me, heal me;
I reinvent myself, I have the power
to release all fears, I have the right
to release all that clings and holds me down
I rise into the light, fresh new and alive;

Guidance

Knowing how much to give and when to give is
important. Do not give what is yours. Do not give
to others and not to the self. Do not place others
above you in importance. Do not, do not.

• • •

Honor yourself, the self you made
Love yourself, the self I have given
Trust yourself, your wisdom lies within
Respect yourself, listen to the messages I send
Treasure all aspects
Those of light and those speckled by the past
Release all into the light;

You are the light of the world
Do not hide your light
You are the salt of creation
You sweeten all you touch
You are my life made manifest
I honor you this day
And all the days to come.

Hold this secret in your heart, dear one
Remember the child that grew
Recall the young girl that triumphed
Know that woman who emerged
In grandeur and in knowing
Oh dear, sweet one, if you could but see yourself
If you could see the flowers at your feet
And free yourself to be
Accepting of all
All will be well
Happy, Happy Birthday!

Dragons

I have entered the cave
seen the dragons
felt their hot, clammy breath,

I have faltered, been afraid
not knowing if I could hold my ground
make my stand
pass by their lair;

I looked, hesitated, took one step
backward, one forward
no progress really, just waiting
contemplating:
"what if…" "what if…"
what will others say?
can I make my pass?

I knew I never would give up
never, never, never…
I held my breath, arched my body
aligned my field, gathered up my strength
let out my "soul-cry"
approached the dragon's lair
saw its glowing eyes and grisly scales
its massive form and blood-flecked claws;

• • •

I shivered, focused my intent,
spread my energetic field
encompassed the great beast
then, suddenly, I was free.

Guidance

Sweet child, look to your past
You have faced the dragon, time and time again
Each time with strong heart
    and with determination
You held your ground, your place
Though the fear roared through your being
You have never given up, but held fast to love
Held fast to hope, held fast to faith
And so you have moved through the gates
Like Innana, stripping away the remnants of earth
Now, you remove the last and final piece

That blocked your way and held you back;

Now you rise and unlike Orpheus
You do not look back
You do not turn back;

You approach the final gate
The final initiation
You make your final stand;

See the light that shines
Hear the music rolling from the hills

Barbara Paul-Emile

Hear the animals rejoice
Hear all creation sing
For you have made the turn for home;

You feel friendless but you have a friend
You feel lonely but behold your company
You feel pained, but behold your joy
You show the wounds, the scars, the breaks,
    the tears
But see the crowning glory,
    the healing wreath of love
Accept your light body, accept the adulation
For you have not failed
You have never stumbled
Nothing was delayed, but all was as it should be
For time waits for you;

Now, you want to disconnect from the world
So strong is your call to the Light
That you are impatient with "worldly things;"

But, fulfill your contract
All things are of light
When rightly seen and understood,
Your crossing is complete
No moment was lost;

Do you know how much I love and honor you?
For the road has not been easy

• • •

And as you exit from the "night"
You feel all that you have experienced;

Talk with me
Stay with me and feel my strength
Take from me
For I freely give to you;
You are never alone
You have never failed
You are tired, yes
For you have undertaken much
These many moons;

But the universe would have you
Release all and let it go
For it is gone;

Those who wronged
But made you stronger
Forgive and release
I give back a thousand fold
The love you thought you lost;

You are my beloved,
You are a part of me,
My essence.

Barbara Paul-Emile

Setting Free

I see, I release, I set free
I am whole, I am healed, I am renewed
I am not earthbound, neither am I attached
to the things of this earth
I am light, I am love, I am joy
I am spirit;

I thank you for ever forgiving me
ever enfolding me in the aegis of your love
    and power
I accept my place and my heritage
I accept my calling and my path
I accept my life;

sometimes I feel that there have been
    more setbacks
    than there should have been
sometimes I feel there has been more confusion
    than there should have been
more unsteadiness than there should have been
more loss of focus
more pain…

but I release the "shoulds" and return to your arms
again, I call on you for strength

• • •

for guidance and for clarity;
Sweet Source, do not forsake me
dusty, bruised and soiled though I might be
my love for you is as ever
my need for you is greater
hear me, this morning as the light streams forth
to awaken all things
let me know that you are there
your beacons beckon
your search-light sprays the land;

my actions have been erratic
but my heart was ever true
fill me with your light
make my wishes come true
bless my words today
as you did yesterday;

Guidance

Every thought and word of yours is heard
I hear you ask for strength, for guidance and
    for clarity
I hear you ask that your wishes and
    desires be answered
And so it is and so it is
They are answered, they are heard.

I give you strength and I give you wisdom
I give you love and I give you comfort
I give you knowing and inner guidance
I give you peace of mind, focus and
    clarity of intent
I give you abundant life, rich with dreams and
    possibilities
I give you your heart's desires
I welcome you home
To the home you never left.

The Past

Know that the past is gone, the future is now
Release the etchings, deep-seated sad memories
Unconsciously carried,
Memories of loss, loneliness, weakness, pain,
    sorrow
Memories of fear, lack and the
    inner-wanting of home
Solidity, firmness, anchoring
The past is gone, quite gone;

Lay these burdens down now
    Accept the you that you are
The child has reached its zenith
Fear nothing;

No one can take what I have given
    No one can offer harm
These threats are but shadowy faces
Read their markings;

Raise your vibrations
Love yourself as
You are loved
You are my light
    You bear no obligation;

Barbara Paul-Emile

Erase past patterns
Make new designations
Release all fears of past or future
They are but shadowy illusions.

Response

I take responsibility for what is not mine
I worry about actions and attitudes
   I cannot change
I grieve for choices others make
I am wounded by the words they say;

I suffer for losses I did not stake
in shadows, doubts intensify the ache
do I define myself by standards others make
always seeking the comfortable place?
these searchings, these wanderings,
I would forego;

Guidance

Give up and walk away
Follow the inner-lighted path.

Treasures

How you are loved!
How you are treasured
Your loyalty, your faith
Your willingness to put your spiritual growth
And path as priorities is commendable
Highly commendable and much admired;

Your soul is repository of our love;
Your life a history of our guidance
You have stood strong through the tests
Now feel our love, our deep and
    abiding love for you;

Do not search for love just feel it for it is poured
    on you
The light surrounds you
Your radiance carries into the dimensions;

Response

I am a lamp, a light burning for my beloved
a pitcher full to slake his thirst
a soil rich and teeming with life energies
I am the starlight that pierces the night,
the beam that fills the day with radiance.

Rejection

You reject me as you reject your roots
    without understanding
You revile me as though I were your enemy
You ignore me as I though I held no meaning
    for you
You shame me as if I were guilty of some
    great crime
You hurt me to show me your power
You throw away my love as though it were useless
    to you
You do not accept my forgiveness
    for it is of no value to you
You give no thanks for the gifts I gave you
You show me how much you despise me
You wish to deprive me of the love of others
You make me know you do not need me;

What harm have I ever done you?
I love you, and I have always cared for you;

Guidance

Do not give away yourself, lady
Do not give yourself, away

. . .

For you are precious and beautiful
Nothing is worth your pain;

Do not humble yourself before them
Do not walk bare-footed on their sharp stones
Do not wear ashes upon your head
Do not look at the face of fear;

Your sweet spirit manifests for all to see
Your goodness runs like streams into the earth,
Your fruits are gentleness, kindness and charity;

Do not hold anguish in your heart
Do not accept their pain
Do not be a receptacle for their torments;

Breathe out into the world your own sweet breath
Like a stream of fire that cleanses, animates
    and heals;

Harden not your heart
Embitter not your thoughts
For they are sacred and precious to me;

They feed my world and nourish all of life
Settle within yourself, detach and know
My love is sufficient.

The Flame

Know that you are beloved beyond all reason
All cause all need and all realization;

You are guarded, protected against all assaults,
    all troubles, all intentions
You are kept ever in the light, in the center of
    the heart of *oneness*
Always guided, loved, treasured,
    wrapped in multiple layers of gossamer strands
    of shimmering light;

Uniqueness...

My breath flows through you
How can I express so that you might understand
That your heart need never be troubled
Need never be bothered
Need never be hurt
Need never be confused or in pain
You need never search, or cry or grieve
Carry regret, or sense of failure
You need never berate yourself reject or criticize;

For you among my daughters are loved
You I hold in my heart
Among your sisters safe and secure;

Feel the flame within   . . .

Feel the assurance building
Feel the tremors of acknowledgement
Feel the greatness of your empowerment;

Know that you are never alone, neglected, rejected
You are never homeless, unsheltered or unloved;

You are the light that brightens the night sky
You are my shimmering water clear and bright
You are the warmth that emanates from the center
Oh! Dear One, you are truly loved.

Response

You have given me great peace
and I am grateful
You have given me great joy
and I am glad
You have held my hand and comforted me
You have surrounded me with light

You have given me the sight
I feel the self
I was meant to be;

You have given me strength
and I have grown
You have whispered to my mind
and it is calm,

Barbara Paul-Emile

You have mentored, loved, guided me
comforted, and protected me
You have poured your wisdom
into my soul
the lines grew straight
the circles whole
the waves flow to the center;

how can I thank You yet again
for your love, your guidance, your presence
how can I tell You yet, again
how central You are to my life?

without You, there is no meaning
no harmony, no joy, no peace and no place
only cracks and broken glass
crooked lines, fragments and decay
let me carry your light within me
let me feel your presence
every moment of the day;

You are the fire that warms
yet never burns
the light that breaks the darkness
the glow among the embers
You are the meaning of the puzzle
the key to every door
the note of every song
my life, my center, my creator.

Spirit Warrior

I am the soldier who rides ever at your side
The guard-protector committed to your defense
The sentry who never sleeps
Always at his post
Never would I leave you
When you are at peace, lady,
I rest.

Response

I draw on your strength spirit-warrior
I draw on your courage, your knowing
your relentless vigilance
I draw on your commitment and on your love
my life rests safely in your hands;

Barbara Paul-Emile

Guidance

You are the emblem on my shield, lady
Strong in your defense

The motto that I carry embolden on my heart;

But I know
Your power lies hidden deep within you
Like the molten center of the earth
Releasing its heat as it slowly rises to the hearth;

I know your true value, lady
I but *appear* to defend you
You need no defense.

The Dance of Life

Your eternal love has been my support. Yes, I have chosen you and do again and again. Give me your strength and your assurance. Give me your love and your support. For all my light I glean from you. All my joys are reflections of your radiance. I dance the dance of life.

the music is your being
I know myself, I know my place
I hold your peace, I feel your grace
I sense your presence and your vibrations
I give myself to their expression.

I draw on your strength, Spirit warrior
I draw on your courage, your relentless vigilance,
    your knowing
I draw on your commitment and on your love
my life rests safely in your hands;

Guidance

You are strong in your own right, woman
Your strength lies hidden within you.

Loving

You are so dearly loved ... so dearly loved
It is a love the depth of which can never be known
For it is the love that holds the universe in place
The earth on course and the streams of life in flow;

Have no regrets, for you have done well
You have walked into dark corners
And have shed your light
You have held your head high and walked alone
You are, indeed, a teacher and a guide
Beloved one, you have shone;

Response

I feel your strength flow through me like
    the current of a river
your winds fill me with the thundering storms
    of heaven
your sun shines as with a geyser's heat
I feel your light surround me like the hallowing of
    the shriven
your presence fills me with the air of
    the high mountain;

I feel your joy embrace me with the freshness of
    sweet remembrances

        • • •

your love stir within me like the liquid light of day
your words echo through me like the murmuring
    of green leaves
I feel my eternal *oneness* with the blossoming
shoots
    of earth
    Inner Teacher, I am grateful;

Though all be taken from me, humbly I accept
    my life
For the losses others bear are greater
I give thanks for my life's wealth: thoughts,
    feelings, yearnings, ambitions, loves searches,
    tears, losses, gains, pains, lessons … LIFE.

The Journey

I am a beacon of love
a holder of the light
a calling of the sea birds
a lashing of the tides;

a shouting from the mountain tops
a beckoning of the breeze
a glowing of the fireflies
a shimmering of the leaves;

I am the tireless traveler
journeying through time
the student, searcher, teacher
finding new paradigms;

my rhythm is my own
the pacing set by soul
I take the curving, winding paths
seeking oneness with the All;

Guidance

You are blessed on your journey
Now and all the days to come
Let peace, timelessness and a loving spirit

• • •

Be your watchwords
Release all fear and pain from your heart
Take my peace;

I am your protector, guardian, guide
I am your armor that shields you from the world
I am the crown you wear
The wings with which you fly
The light of knowingness that settles in the heart
I am the voice with which you speak
The pen that translates my words
The sweet spirit that cushions your soul
I am your only goal.

Barbara Paul-Emile

DISCOVERING THE
AUTHENTIC SELF

Come Away with Me

Come with me away from the chaos and the din
Come with me away from the noise and
   the confusion
Come with me to where it is quiet
And you are truly valued;

Come with me away from those
   who would take from you
And withhold their giving
Come away with me from duality in all its forms
Come away with me from uncertainty and fear;

Come, come quickly for the light fades
And the cries can be heard,
You have no place here
You never had, you never will;

Your place is with me
For you have chosen many years ago
Your place is at my side
That place for you is held;

Do not travel from place to place

Looking, seeking, searching
You have found your joy, your peace

. . .

Do not care about what will be said
    when you leave
You will not be missed;

The light you carry obscures their vision
It creates but a flash of memory
Others chose not to see.

Barbara Paul-Emile

Intrinsic Worth

Until you learn to trust, love and honor yourself
Until you release all attention to outward
    validation
And understand your worth is intrinsic
Until you fearlessly center the search within and
    not without
Until you cease to live without and create
    a different reality
They are your teachers;

There is really nothing that they can offer you
Give you or withhold from you;

Their approval cannot elevate or demean you
Their treatment of you reflect themselves, not you
Release them from your scope or focus
They have served their purpose;

Now rise above it all
Heal and love yourself
We are always here with you.

Mastership

A master knows when to give and
    when to withhold
When to be with others and when to be alone
When to hold on and when to let go
When to be active and when to be at peace;

A master knows no power over others
    but power over himself
A master knows when to accept responsibility and
    when to relinquish it
A master does not condemn others;

A master finds peace in all things
    knowing all is in its rightful place
A master knows that life is a laboratory
    for learning
And lavishes love not only on others but
    on himself
A master recognizes hurtful patterns and
    changes them
A master listens within and walks between
    dimensions.

Barbara Paul-Emile

Meditation on Obligation

Free yourself from obligation
Obligation to anyone
Obligation to a perceived self;

I made you free
Unique, individual, inviolate;

Honor this before you move
To change, to distort, to fit
Established molds;

I made you free
Do not give the self I made away
To anyone;

Hold my expression pure and true,
    Hold!

On Trusting

Trust yourself this day
And all the days to come...
Trust your hunches, feelings, insights
Place no authority before you
Look not back to what is passed;

Know my wisdom speaks through you
My guidance comes to light your way
    Trust yourself always
In all you do and all you say;

Be at peace with your decisions
Decisions taken from the heart
Decisions taken in the silence
Decisions reached through inner prompting
Decisions that bring peace to the soul;

Be at peace with your choices
    Your past, your future, whatever is to come
Move forward in the center of your path
    Full of inner knowing

Barbara Paul-Emile

Remember this path is your own and no other
    Each entity sparkles as it will
Taking unique form and shape
    I abide in you forever
Erasing, loving, teaching, coaching, guiding;

You are not alone

Hear my voice
Tend to my ways
Flow in peace and grace
    Hear me now:
            Breathe and be at rest.

Cleansing

I cleanse and I renew myself
I walk through the fire trough
purged by its searing heat
healed by its radiance;

I stand beneath the roaring waterfall
feel the splashing on my body
feel the washing of Spirit
and know that I am whole.

Barbara Paul-Emile

Old Shirts

Release these feelings like old shirts
Outgrown, outworn, no longer useful
Let them go
You have outgrown this confining space;

I say to you:
Know that the past and all it held is gone
In this new day
All your clothing is newly made
Sown by spirit
Your light garments absorb all sorrows and fears
Their seams hold
And your safety is assured
Your balance is restored
Your challenges faced and won
The fabric of your life
Sown with care and with love;

Don your new garments
Walk forth with confidence
Knowing that I AM
Designer and seamstress,
Both.

Fearing

Fearing to live, we die in pieces
we dam our energies, here and there
clutter life with useless odds and ends
pull back in denial, rejections, fears …

we repeat "no" to ourselves
"I can't" becomes a litany
we look outside for answers, guidance, light…

where are the authority figures, books, guidelines?
who will tell us this or that is OK
while this or that is not?

can we trust ourselves?
can we follow our own principles, inner guidance?
dare we say "Yes, we know"?

but what will others say?

Barbara Paul-Emile

The Critic

Put away the critic
Turn his face to the wall
For he is not needed now
His work is done, his time is past
No one can judge you now;

Who has the right, the knowledge, the vision?
To whom are you beholden?
Who condemns you, measures you, assesses you?
To whom are you beholden?

They but assess themselves
They but see themselves and never you
So, free your consciousness,
    your thoughts and actions
See, breathe, feel only me
And I do not judge you.

The Unseen Ones

You are so loved, so cherished and so cared for
Do not weep and do not worry
For we, the unseen ones, are always here for you
At your beck and call;

Simply tell us your wishes and demands
And they will be carried out
We are here to help you
Assist, love and sustain you
So, do not weep
Let nothing break your heart
No perceived rejection or violation
You are never alone
Never!
We are always here.

Spend more time with us
In our company
Call upon us more
Wander not so far away;

For like the dew we rise in the morning
Like the sun we shed our light
Like the wind our currents surround you
Like the rain we nourish and restore you

Barbara Paul-Emile

We are yours,

    We are you!

When you feel alone
It is because you have turned away

We cannot be replaced in your life
For all things rest in us
We are you, dear, lady,
        We are you!

Create a World

Create a world for yourself
A world of peace and harmony
A world in which you dwell apart
A world where all is heightened beauty
Color and dance,
Create for yourself, a space
Private and sacred
Where none can enter
Unless invited
Where you can be at peace
And in full acceptance;

Do not absorb the painful searchings of others
Do not seek to know all
    the "whys" and "wherefores"
Threads from ten thousand spools
Create the texture of life;

You are not asked to be responsible for the world
You are asked to live in it in peace.

Barbara Paul-Emile

Unchartered Lands

He thought he'd plumbed the bottom of my well,
knew my straight and narrow paths
my thicket and my barren lands
my peaks and valleys, mapped and planned;

he did not know my silent springs,
my subterranean risings,
my streams of gushing water pure
secret mines, rich with precious store,

landscape, unchartered fresh and green
he did not know, for he had not seen.

Green Fields

Your life has been like a green, green field
To which all creatures come
To feed and be replenished;

Your life has been like a fresh, clear stream
To which many come to drink and be refreshed;

Your life has been like a snow-capped mountain
Triumphant and magnificent in its being;

Your life has been like a bridge
Connecting worlds that were apart;

Your life is a never-ending journey
Ever moving forward in its knowing;

Your life...

Your life has been a precious stone
Rich with its inner beauty,
Your life has been a beacon
Guiding those lost at sea,
Your anchor resting at great depths
Holds them firm, yet free;

Barbara Paul-Emile

I know you look for meaning
And you do not fully understand
I know you see your circles
And wonder where will your rotation end;

But fear not, Woman,
Know that you have traveled great distances
The knowledge you've gained lies deep within you
Like ore in the body of the earth
You have blended and absorbed this knowledge
So that you no longer see its prints
But be assured, dear lady,
You have learned, you have grown
And you have shone.

The Circle

I hold to my faith and to this honored path
I call from the depth of my being
I call to echo down the corridors of time
through the silences of the ages;

I call to the sprays of light
Triggering that first pale dawn
I call to swing wide the great gates
To unfurl the flags
To sound the trumpets
To give shouts of joy,
    and of praise-song
for I know,
    I know who I am;

I hear my voice among the throng
I know my place of origin
I affirm my constancy, my inner being
I hold my place
    my place within the Circle.

Barbara Paul-Emile

Sovereignty

Like clear, clear streams, we glow to the light
   like clear, clear streams, we shimmer in
   luminescence;

like clear, clear streams, we become one with spirit
for we have crossed the stormy waters
felt the wind shriek and howl at our backs
felt the saltines and acidity on our tongues;

we have faced death and fear
   terrible and threatening
we have cried and called for help…
and have become by turns angry and despairing;

we have murmured "why?"
we have cursed and we have prayed;

and then…

we grew strong
we began to hold our ground
we turned to face the gales, tasted the waters
and felt our powers,

we felt our strength rise and eddy within
   we began to know ourselves
we began to feel the fullness of our presence;

• • •

The Dance of Life

for...
out of fear comes understanding
out of understanding comes love and acceptance
out of acceptance comes peace;

we have risen from the ashes of our own burning
the flames bright and fierce flashed 'round us
we felt not the heat but the light
not the pain but the glory

for...
transmutation brings knowledge
transmutation returns us to the self;

settled within our own center
we feel safe, secure and at peace;

we know the power of the center
we know the raging of the storm
we know the pain of self-rejection
we know the memory of the past hurts;

but, all hurts heal
all storms become still
all learning leads to growth

and...
all growth leads to knowing.

Barbara Paul-Emile

HONORING THE TAO OF LIFE

Welcoming Oona...

A spark of light
resting in a tiny form

so delicate, yet so strong

so wonderfully made
so lovingly detailed
so beautiful in her perfection

her radiance, the sparkle of a dewdrop
her presence, the softness of evening
her cry, the life-force of the universe

so eager to grow and to become
Oona, our Joy, the Centered One.

Mist Mountain

Like a pure, clear stream
   from Maine's high mountains
carrying its waters shining in the sun
sparkling 'neath blue skies and green vistas
shimmering, rippled beads in the mountain breeze
knowing itself, flowing to the sea;

So do I on this hazy, misty morning
wet with the night's rain
feel the call to reverence and to silence
turn my heart to the cloud-covered mountains
knowing myself part of All-That-Is
knowing myself part of the rain and of the mist
feeling my spirit flowing to the great sea
the Great Sea of Life.

Barbara Paul-Emile

Morning Sea

There is a power and a serenity in
    the morning sea
sprinkled with light, rippled with delicate
patterns,
light, glass-like, reflecting and refracting on
its surface
the wind gently lifting at its foaming caps
Seagulls on the wing
early strollers breaking the cold, gray sand;

I feel at home here
fearing neither rocks nor sea nor sand
accepting the quiet, letting it flow through me
accepting the peace, letting it still my mind
releasing my fears;

The morning sea is glorious in its calm beauty
playful, gentle, welcoming
all is quiet before the day is come;

Spirits beckon us to awaken with the light
come forth and feel this sweet tranquility
keep it with us through all the days to come
this time, this moment, this morning.

Incoming Tide—Ogunquit

Land, crimped, scratchy, hard,
showing its sandy surface to the sky,
patterned, marked, shaped, re-claimed,
stretched out away to meet the rising ocean;

We walk, smiling our pleasure,
picking up mussel shells along the shore,
listening to the husky rustling of the water
feeling the whispering, curling of the wind
around ourselves;

Then slowly, soundlessly, the water begins its
inward journey,
inching, creeping over sand and
stone,
inward, ever inward, towards the shore;

Relentless in its undulating surges
powerful foaming waves
release gentle-moving currents,
each receding to give the other life
as the water returns to the land it has known
to the paths that bring it home;

Barbara Paul-Emile

The land accepts the incoming tide
steadies the waters as it eddies in its wake
holds its tumultuous power with an easy grace;

Knowing this must be, as does all else
the tide is in, the waters roll
I hold its power for the allotted time
the patterns change, yet I am still the same
I am land and will be again.

Island Memories

Am I destined to be alone
without ancestral ones around me
no furrowed brow to kiss
lined hand to touch?

Lines that tell of shared past
    and of origins…
words that tell of beginnings
    and days gone by
when stories were links
    of days strung out like leaves;

Where are the memories
of childhood days spent
threading four-o'clocks on strings
drinking water from conch shells
catching crayfish in net baskets
lodged between wet legs,
eating bammy cakes and codfish
goat stew hot with relish
scented fever grass and guinep
sugar cane and jack fruit?

Where are my childhood songs, verses, rhymes
texts of sermons lovingly recalled?

Barbara Paul-Emile

where are the wild birds
bad boys tried to catch
sling shots behind stone walls?

Where are the ones who knew my name
names others do not know or else forgot?

Where are the calls of milkmen on their rounds?
pedlers soldering pots sitting on the ground?
where are the fried fish, june-plums,
soursops and scented lime trees?
sound of lone trucks whining in the dust?

Where are the ones who made me safe?
who with their word created for me a world
where shadows pointed to the light
    gave my first memorable gift:
    a pen with which to write.

The Garden

Come forward, this day
For the garden is wet with rain
The earth is fertile with its riches
The scents alive with fragrance
Come forth this day and play;

Come forward and see
See the light shining through the trees
See the birds resting on the branches
See the butterfly resting on the leaf;

Nature and its world invite you to come forth
See the flowers waving gently in the wind
See the weeds daring to offer up their green shoots
See the stones, billions of years new
See all that is here for you;

Come into the garden
For I am the gardener and the farmer
I plant all that is planted
The earth is wet and moist with dew
Its crystals glitter on the petals;

Come feel your oneness with All-That-Is
Feel your energies flow out to the earth
Feel the center shift unto its hold
The scent of the garden is sweet and compelling
The voice of the gardener holds you enthralled;

Barbara Paul-Emile

You fear the thorns
You fear the branches
Your fear the windy nature of the path
But fear not, traveler
For this is your garden, your earth
You are one with all things here;

Do not turn away for separateness
Join the unity of earth
Take your place here in this garden
Join your energies with this new growth;

Take but a step into the garden
Make a movement to begin
Hold but the thought within your mind
And all the clarion bells will ring
And all nature rise to greet you.

The Brothers

The brothers serving, peaceful, kind
Defy the vagaries of time
Cling steadfast to their faith;

Centered, knowing, steady, strong
They keep the night-watch of the soul;

Sentinels, clarions, guardians of the
    flame
Their silent call issues forth again:

    to heal the spirit, the heart, the soul
    to revive and to make whole
    to reform and to restore
    that which time has badly torn

Where are their accolades of praise?
Their profits, tallies, returns and fees?
Their names written down for all to see?

Inner Joy!

Barbara Paul-Emile

Gifts to Welcome Strangers

Every word a jewel
every sound a call
silence echoes like the opening of a
flower
beauty, grace, contemplation
there is nothing more.

Retreat: The Soul's Journey

Chants, private thoughts and silences
time out from constructs of the world
reach back to origins and to completions
forward to beginnings and to progressions
we gather strength for one more pass at life
we stretch ourselves to span the
    bridge of time...

To touch eternity...

    Glastonbury Abbey.

Barbara Paul-Emile

The Race

Like a streak of light glowing and effervescing
like a whisp of wind darting swiftly
   through the leaves
like a flash of thought here and then gone
like the flight of a bird pathless and free
     may you rise up out of your blocks
             courage in your heart
             strength in your feet
poised like a bird for flight
poised like a leopard for the sprint
                away you fly
       feeling the joy of the motions
feeling the flow of energy to your limbs
       feeling the glory of the race

We run with you, dear daughter, to be lost
in the silence of your running
in the symphony of your rhythms
in the cadences of unheard shouts and screams
in the pounding of your heartbeat
in the flow of wingéd feet

    We too feel
  the wind against our faces
the straining of muscle and tendon
the pain-joy of pushing past limits

                • • •

We too feel
the triumphant surge of power
to pass the competition
to reach into the beyond...

We honor you this day, daughter
for your magnificent courage
your incontrovertible desire to excel
your love for your sport
your power, your longing
your perfect dedication.

The 200

In track as in life
you fly out of your blocks
build up speed
run a tight, hard curve
leaning in…
take the lead
and hold it;

Then,
powering down the straight
straining for the finish line
pushing… pressing… leaning…
you give it your all
and cross it:

Champion!

Mosaic

She is the sun that warms the coming day
the rustling wind that will not stay

she is the cry of young birds on the wing
the roar of gushing waters in the springs

the fragrant pine tree tall and straight
shaken by storms, holds and does not break

the silence of deep, icy Nordic oceans
the purr of tropic mountain streams

she is the scent of fresh cut grass in spring
the feel of summer's moist brown earth

the melting heat of hot July
the crispness of cold December

she is sweetness, pain, joy and laughter
a girl, a woman, a friend, a daughter

a kaleidoscope of dazzling colors:

Mosaic.

Barbara Paul-Emile

Advent

I reached out a hand to touch, to stroke her back
as I was wont to do
my child, my daughter, newly affianced;

I felt her lover's auric shield
tangible, evident, like a cloak
a mantle, an encircling beam
strong, protective and unyielding;

He did not turn to touch her
yet I knew his touch was still upon her
the pulsing, magnetic field 'round her now
was his, not mine;

I stayed my hand and did not break
the web of this deep caring
this barrier of his love;

For then I knew:

This was the advent of her life
a claim not to be denied
she was now encircled by another's field
other bondings had been sealed;

Sudden knowing, laughter and surprise
she was child, now grown daughter
        and will be wife.

My Beloved

You taught me how to love you
and you showed me how
you touched my heart, my soul, my inner being
and said: "Such is my love for you;"

You took me in safe-keeping
held me close, cherished and protected me
swore faith with me
and kept your word;

Adorned me generously with love's jewels
with luster that will not fade
nor brightness dim
nor radiance pale;

You showed me how to be fearless in my giving
to walk unarmed into the battlefields of life
knowing I was armored with your love;

You are my love, my life-stream
my strong high beam
that keeps my foundation sure.

Barbara Paul-Emile

Goodbyes

Goodbyes are always sad
for they linger in the heart
like a note that never stops
like bells that always chime
like mountains always to be climbed;

Goodbyes are always sad
for they fragment the soul
break apart the whole
tear life into little pieces;

Goodbyes are always sad,
like water dripping in a cistern
like mourning sounds carried on the breeze
muffled cries none can hear but me;

Goodbye is like a solitary leaf
hanging on a tree
when all have fallen to the ground
flutters back and forth and waits the winter.

Doves of Peace

The grief, the pain, the feelings of despair
the refusal to accept the truth
that you are now beyond my reach
you have made your choice
you have chosen another path;

To weep, to allow the pain
    to encircle and engulf
to sense the feelings of loss
    betrayal and abandonment;

To accept the unacceptable
to acknowledge the reality
you are closing this chapter
you are beginning another;

I cry as heralds do
to warn of pitfalls, traps and cliffs
I scream my pain;

I feel the break
I turn to walk away
knowing the time has come
    to assess the past
        to make the future
            to release in love
            to accept the pain
To let fly the doves of peace.

Barbara Paul-Emile

In Memoriam

When great ones come among us
  they seldom stay for long;
glowing, radiant, incandescent,
  they illuminate the world
            we see their form
            join in their song
but their spirits are forever free
  Such a one was she;

Young, poised, indefatigably strong:
  scholar, athlete, artist, friend
what powers she did display…
  beauty, intellect and grace
her life, a dazzling interface;

She lived the cycle of a day,
  each hour the fullness of a year;

We who knew and loved her dear,
  hold in our hearts and do not forget
that once there was a sylph, a seraph, a star,
  whose radiance touched the earth;

She danced a shimmering moment
  on the land

• • •

weaving sacred patterns in the sand
sprinkling stardust with her hands

Then...
spiraling out of time
was gone...

Beloved friend, we do remember you...
Rita!

Clearing

There is a logic to clearing drawers
throwing out papers, used and forgotten

There is a reason to clear desks and files
putting aside what has already given of itself;

There is a purpose, there is a logic
there is a reason for everything…

We clear our minds, our hearts, our souls
we give ourselves a chance to start again
we accept the unacceptables
cast aside the imponderables
it is good business, it is life and it is growth.

Sweet Wisdom

May I know when to say yes
   and when to say no
when to hold on
   and when to let go;

May I know when to give
   and when to withhold
when to move forward
   and when to be still;

May I know the true meaning of things
   may I learn how to live.

Time! Time! Time!

Time is but a construct
grided to control
    a convention created
breaking up the whole;

Time is a narrow roadway
linear in its design
    pushing ever forward
precipitous in its incline;

Time is society's imprimatur
celled to separate
    a sectioning of nature
a breaking of the flow;

yet,

Time is malleable and giving
discover its secret ways
    now fast-paced, timorous, now slow
responding to our days;

Time does not control us
it is an elaborate scheme

. . .

calendars, clocks, palm-pilots
we control their destiny;

for,

Time is one aspect of the stream
timelessness flows by its side
    calm, peaceful, knowing
the one to choose?
you must decide.

The choice is a spiritual journey
one we freely take;

But for me?
I release grids and time-locks
I choose the timeless flow.

Dismissing Time

Open your heart to me
Let me crown your head with glory
Let me heal the bruises and the pain
Let me hold you in my embrace
Let me remind you that you are loved
No bandit can lay-in-wait
No mine-traps subvert your path;

For I protect and keep that which is mine
I do not become careless and forget
I do not lay aside and reject
I do not wander off and leave you alone
To face hardships and be afraid;

I love you, my life flows through you
You are of my retinue
Feel my presence,
Know that "I am here."
And where I am, no harm comes
No anger, fears or jealousies abide
For I have dismissed Time.

Patience

Do not answer unless you are called
Do not give unless you are asked
Do not speak unless you'll be heard
Spread your love and care like buttered bread
To those who desire it.

TRANSCENDENCE

Light Streams

You are the light of my soul
the streams that flow through my being
you are the essence that burns at the core
the sweetness that flows from every pore
you are life, love, meaning, focus and goal
you are All-That-Is.

Connection

Those who would replenish their inner stores
Give readily and fully looking not for return
Water the parched lands with their love
Throw out their warm cloak
    to enfold the cold and lost
Open their hearts to the needy and destitute
Welcome home the weary and the forsaken
These hearts beat in unison with All-That-Is
To keep this earth on its turn.

Barbara Paul-Emile

Banners in the Wind

Fear not, for the dangers have past
The long night is gone, the winds subside
The light is come, the morning breaks
Feel the glow and splendor of the sun;

You have carried your banner well
You have withstood the darkness and the flood
You have been shaken by the turmoil and the rain
Never faltering, never looking back again;

For your pledge you had given
Your promise you had made
Love held you loyal
Faith kept you there;

You surrendered to the spirits
Opened wide your heart
Held fast to your knowing
Dangers could not shake;

Stood in your strength
Freed yourself from pain
Exorcised your fears
Braced in the cold, cold air;

See the colors of the morning
Feel the warmth of this new dawn

. . .

Stand in the glow of incandescence
Know your oneness with the earth
See the streaming of the light
Feel yourself alive after the long night;

You are that radiance, woman,
You are that light.

Magnificence

See, know, notice and record
What magnificent beings you are;

Notice your tenacity
Record your faithfulness
Record your generosity and your kindness
See the fruit of love's labors
See your struggles and your triumphs
See your endurance and your reward;

Know these things are seen and recorded;

Your life has had its share of hardships
Now enjoy your triumph
Enjoy your overcoming
Enjoy your time of surrender
For we bring you gifts, rich and splendid
Bright with colors, sweet with scents
Burgundies, deep ruby reds, dark and sweet;

Your gifts await you
We know your needs
Heart treasures, balanced and aligned
For a jewel, priceless and sublime.

Whenever

I feel you close, ever so close
whenever I see shadows,
    you shed the light of truth
whenever I fear for the future,
    you cradle and support
whenever I condemn myself,
    you comfort and reassure
whenever I feel I've failed,
    you show me my successes
whenever I feel abandoned,
    you tell me of my safety
whenever I wander far away,
    you gently call me home
whenever, whenever, whenever...

You are there.

Barbara Paul-Emile

New Day...

You have awakened from your sleep,
You have thrown off the covers,
Pushed open the windows of your life
Felt the warm sun shine upon your skin
The breeze upon your face
The rustling of the trees
Smelled the sweetness of fresh flowers
Seen the birds soaring in the skies
And have known that a new day has come.

New Guides

Tip your sails to the wind of life
Feel my flow
Unfurl and lean into the wind
Let it carry you out
Floating, effortless before the sweep of waves
Tack neither to the left nor to the right
Stay the course
For I will guide;

Call forth the new spirit
That will manifest in you
Thank and free the soul that carried you here
Release and let it go
At this moment and in this time
You need to create anew;

Welcome the spirit that comes to take its place
Welcome her and speak not of the past
For it is gone;

Watch her new ways
See her choose fresh paths
Relax for she is vigilant
Know that you have traveled far along this path;

Your heart is open
Your spirit strong and free
Your goals achieved
Your sight illumined
In this we are agreed
Rest for she is centered.

Hallowed Morning

You are my essence, my true self
you are my purpose and my goal
you are the health of my body, mind and spirit
you are the joy, the silence and
    the truth that I seek;

For I have pledged to you long ago
long ago I heard your call
long ago I took it to my heart
under your aegis, I have lived my life;

I have fallen, stumbled, sat by the roadside
I have lost my way at times
so it would appear
as I have worried about *when* and *how* and *why;*

But you have ever been true to me
ever faithful, ever loving, ever kind
in the halo of your caring love
I am healed, restored, replenished
and made new;

Barbara Paul-Emile

On this momentous morning
I choose to see the world that you would
  have me see
I choose to value what you have taught is worthy

I choose to release
  to be the self you would have me be
and so it is.

Totems

May we be nourished by spirit
   may we never be in want
may there always be sufficient
may we be loved and guided,
   may we dwell in safety
may we contribute to the good of the world
may we do no harm upon this planet
   may we grow in light and truth
may we be part of earth's great web of peace.

Breaking Free

Know that you are loved
Beyond all things
Loved beyond all counting
And beyond measure;

Break through and free yourself
Step through
Claim Your Birthright
Take Your Freedom

Join the *Oneness*.

Transcendence

I have changed and I have become
I have held my place, steadied my feet
known my strengths
faced my weaknesses
heard the repetition of my cries…

discerned the fears that trouble me
the anxieties that extinguish my inner fires
the childhood histories that haunt and weaken
the inner strength that rises unbidden
keeping me safe, sure and certain;

the energies have shifted
past patterns are released
with this new understandings rise
my vision clear, my self-concept deepens;

I know myself more fully
trust myself, nor fear to leave the path
I am anchored deep within the well of eternity
my essence rests easy in the center of stillness;

Barbara Paul-Emile

the clouds clear
the sun rises
the dawn breaks

its colors spray the earth
and I rise with it
for it is morning
my morning on the earth,
certainty, triumph, graduation!

ABOUT THE AUTHOR

Barbara Paul-Emile was born and raised in Springfield, a district ten miles from Montego Bay, Jamaica. She has written creatively since childhood. To her, poems have always been a way of connecting with the world, a way of coming to terms with life in its rich complexity, of finding the essence, the truth within experience. Described as "an exciting new literary voice who chronicles the richness of multicultural experience," Professor Paul-Emile has recently published a new novel, *SEER,* which tells a magical tale of redemption set against the lush landscape and spicy aromas of the Caribbean.

A Professor of English and Maurice E. Goldman Distinguished Professor of Arts and Sciences, at Bentley College, Waltham, Massachusetts, Professor Paul-Emile received her BA (Phi Beta Kappa) and MA from New York University and her Ph.D. in English from the University of Colorado, Boulder. She has taught at the University of Colorado, Boulder, Vassar College, Brandeis University, Boston University and was a fellow and associate director at the Radcliffe Institute for Post Doctoral Studies, Harvard University.

Her work centers on 19th century English Romantic Poets, Caribbean literature, and African-American literatures. This breadth allows her to combine her interest in myth/folklore, third world literature with her knowledge of European colonial literary influences. Although Paul-Emile has published numerous articles on scholarly topics, creative writing—especially poetry—remains close to her heart. Professor Paul-Emile has received many teaching and scholarly awards and her contribution to her field was recognized at the national level when, in 1995, she was named Massachusetts Professor of the Year by the Carnegie Foundation and the Council for the Advancement and Support of Education.

CPSIA information can be obtained
at www.ICGtesting.com
Printed in the USA
LVHW091748130819
627498LV00001B/2/P